AFTER JESUS

DISCOVER *the* HOLY SPIRIT

AFTER JESUS

DISCOVER *the* HOLY SPIRIT

H.L. STADLER

MARCELLUS & CASSIAN

Published by Marcellus & Cassian

www.marcellusandcassian.com

Unless otherwise stated, Scripture quotations taken from the King James Version, public domain.

ISBN: 979-8-9883300-0-4

ISBN (E-Book): 979-8-9883300-1-1

Printed in the United States of America

"Until the spirit be poured upon us from on high, and the wilderness be a fruitful field, and the fruitful field be counted for a forest. . . . Blessed are ye that sow beside all waters."

— ISAIAH 32:15,20

"Ho, every one that thirsteth, come ye to the waters, and he that hath no money; come ye, buy, and eat; yea, come, buy wine and milk without money and without price.

Wherefore do ye spend money for that which is not bread? and your labour for that which satisfieth not? hearken diligently unto me, and eat ye that which is good, and let your soul delight itself in fatness."

— ISAIAH 55:1-2

CONTENTS

Preface i

1 / Born of the Spirit **1**

2 / The Father's Promise **9**

3 / Fulfillment of the Promise **19**

4 / The Sign **27**

5 / The Great Significance **37**

6 / Our Helper **49**

7 / Extinguishing the Spirit **67**

8 / The Seal **75**

9 / Open the Gift **83**

PREFACE

The Bible wasn't written to be understood just by scholars or pastors; it was written to be understood by everyone. Nurses, carpenters, plumbers, accountants, cooks, janitors, maids, soldiers, and fishermen, just to name a few, are called to personally understand it. Even if you don't have an occupation, God is no respecter of persons. He longs to teach you and reveal to you the Scriptures.

In his first letter to the Corinthians, Paul wrote that the spiritual person can evaluate everything. If you are a son or a daughter of God through Jesus Christ, you can understand what God desires to speak to you through His Word.

I will refrain from adding many of my words and allow the Scriptures to lead and speak for themselves. Like the Bereans, let's be open-minded and search the Scriptures to see if what I write is true. Because the Bereans "received the word with all readiness, and searched the Scriptures daily to find out whether these things were so," many of them received eternal life (Acts 17:11-12).

It is our responsibility to analyze and examine what others say and write and then compare it to the Bible. God is faithful to reveal to us the truth. If we dig in the Word for the foundation of our beliefs, we will gain a clear understanding of God's plan and expectations for our lives.

I

BORN OF THE SPIRIT

"For as many as are led by the Spirit of
God, they are the sons of God."

— ROMANS 8:14

THE BOOK OF ACTS CHAPTER EIGHT TELLS US OF AN
evangelist named Phillip who traveled to a city in
Samaria. Upon arrival, he preached the gospel
and cast out evil spirits. Through him, God healed many
paralyzed and lame people. Great joy filled the people of
the city, and many believed that Jesus is Lord and were
baptized in water.

Over in Jerusalem, the apostles heard about this wonderful news and sent Peter and John to pray for these
new believers so that they might receive the Holy Spirit.
Why did the apostles do this? After all, these Samaritans

already believed the gospel and were baptized. What else could they need?

Let's read what happened. "Now when the apostles which were at Jerusalem heard that Samaria had received the word of God, they sent unto them Peter and John: Who, when they were come down, *prayed for them, that they might receive the Holy Ghost:* (For *as yet* he was fallen upon none of them: only they were baptized in the name of the Lord Jesus.) Then laid they their hands on them, and *they received the Holy Ghost*" (Acts 8:14-17; emphasis added). These men and women were saved and baptized in the name of the Lord Jesus (water baptism), yet they were still missing something or rather, some*one* falling upon them. Acts 8:17 doesn't say they received a gift from the Holy Spirit, it says they received *Him*.

The apostles valued the act of the Holy Spirit falling upon a believer so greatly that they sent Peter and John all the way from Jerusalem to pray for them. One must ask why. After all, since these men and women were indeed saved and thus had the Holy Spirit, how come they needed to be prayed over to receive Him?

So, I continued to study the Word. As a result, the Bible revealed a difference between being *born* of the Spirit and being *filled* with the Spirit.

BORN AGAIN OF THE SPIRIT

God created our bodies to carry our spirits here on Earth. We are more than just dust; we are spirits and our spirits came from the Lord. In John 3, Jesus said that unless we are born again, we cannot see the kingdom of God.

When Nicodemus heard this, he asked Him, "How can a man be born when he is old? Can he enter the second time into his mother's womb, and be born?" (John 3:4).

Jesus replied, "Except a man be born of water and of the Spirit, he cannot enter into the kingdom of God. That which is born of the flesh is flesh; and that which is born of the Spirit is spirit" (John 3:5-6).

You are a spirit being who has a soul and lives in a body. If you were a simply a human body, you would need to return to your mother's womb and be born again. But Jesus said that if you are born of the Spirit, you are a spirit.

Ephesians 4:24 says, "And that ye put on *the new man*, which after God is created in righteousness and true holiness" (emphasis added). When you became a new man or woman in Christ Jesus, your physical body did not transform into a baby or a different form. You still possessed the same eye and hair color. You still weighed the same and bore the same lines on your face. That's because your new man, which is your spirit, became new, righteous, and holy, not your body. Your spirit was born again by the Holy Spirit through Jesus' death and resurrection.

Jesus said, "A spirit hath [has] not flesh and bones" (Luke 24:39). Desiring to leave the Earth to be with the Lord, Paul wrote, "For I am in a strait betwixt two, having a desire to depart, and to be with Christ; which is far better: Nevertheless to abide *in the flesh* is more needful for you" (Philippians 1:23-24; emphasis added). Paul knew he was first a spirit, which is why he wrote that he'd rather remain in his body for the church's benefit. When he eventually departed the Earth, it was him (his spirit) that left to be together with the Lord. In the same way, when God calls us to Him, our spirits will depart our bodies to be with Him.

Many people confuse their souls to be their spirits, when in fact they are two distinct entities. Hebrews 4:12 says, "For the word of God is quick, and powerful, and sharper than any twoedged sword, piercing even to the *dividing asunder of soul and spirit*" (emphasis added). If soul and spirit are the same thing, how can they be divided?

A person's soul holds their mind and emotions. They

can be born again in their spirit and be troubled and wounded in their soul at the same time. Many Christians are whole in their spirits and have assurance of salvation, but their souls are broken from past experiences and decisions.

David wrote in Psalm 23:3, "He [God] restoreth my soul." While the spirit is re-birthed, the soul is restored. Like an old piece of furniture restored to its original beautiful state, our soul's restoration depends on our continual obedience to God's Word (James 1:21-25, Rom. 12:1-2). Paul's prayer for the church was that their "whole spirit, soul, and body be preserved blameless at the coming of our Lord Jesus Christ" (1 Thessalonians 5:23).

Christ said, "It is the spirit that quickeneth; the flesh profiteth nothing: the words that I speak unto you, they are spirit, and they are life" (John 6:63). Because the Holy Spirit gives life, He must be present in physical *and* spiritual creation. The same Holy Spirit who first created us holds the power to re-birth our spirits through our faith in Jesus Christ.

Adam's body was a hollow shell until God gave it the breath of life. When Adam sinned, his spirit and therefore, our spirits became corrupt with sin and destined for eternity without God. The only way for us to be redeemed is to be born again. It is by the conviction and action of the Holy Spirit that God makes us His children. When we are born again, we are born of, by, and through the Spirit of God.

The Bible declares that no one can say, "Jesus is Lord" except by the Holy Spirit. So, when Jesus asked His disciples who they said He was, Peter replied, "Thou art the Christ, the Son of the living God" (Matthew 16:16). By the Holy Spirit, Peter said that Jesus is Lord.

In John 20:21, after He resurrected, Jesus breathed on His disciples and told them to receive the Holy Spirit. Peter received the Holy Spirit from Jesus while He was still on Earth. First Corinthians 15:14 says, "And if Christ has not been raised, our preaching is *useless* and *so is your faith*," (emphasis added). Peter couldn't have been born again in his spirit by the Holy Spirit without Jesus' resurrection.

Likewise, when we are born again, we receive the Holy Spirit. When we give our lives to Christ, the Holy Spirit makes His home with us, leading us as children of God into all the Lord has prepared for us. But as Jesus specified to the disciples in John 14:17, "He [the Holy Spirit] dwelleth *with* you, and shall be *in* you" (emphasis added).

After Jesus breathed on the disciples to receive the Holy Spirit, He also commanded them to wait in Jerusalem for a certain promise. In Luke 24:49, Jesus said, "And, behold, I send the promise of my Father upon you: but tarry ye in the city of Jerusalem, until ye be endued with power from on high."

Jesus' instructions to the disciples reveals four things. First, at one or multiple points in history, their heavenly Father gave them a promise. Secondly, Jesus revealed that it was He who would send it. Thirdly, they'd receive it if they waited in Jerusalem. Lastly, when it would come upon them, they would receive God's power.

These disciples had spent three years learning alongside the Son of God, yet they still needed to receive this promise. After Jesus ascended to Heaven, one hundred and twenty believers would wait in Jerusalem for it. And per Jesus' commandment, they could not take another step beyond the city until He poured it out.

2

THE FATHER'S PROMISE

"This Jesus hath God raised up, whereof
we all are witnesses. Therefore being
exalted, and having received of the Father
the promise of the Holy Ghost, he hath
shed forth this, which ye now see and
hear."

— Acts 2:32-33

In Joel 2:28-29, God promised through the prophet Joel, "And it shall come to pass afterward, that I will pour out my spirit upon all flesh; and your sons and your daughters shall prophesy, your old men shall dream dreams, your young men shall see visions: And also upon the servants and upon the handmaids in those days will I pour out my spirit."

God spoke of a time where all His sons and daughters,

old and young, would receive the outpouring of the Holy Spirit. In the Old Testament, many prophets told of the coming Messiah in Psalm 22 and Isaiah 14 and 53 to name a few. When Jesus Christ came to Earth, He fulfilled every prophecy. Here, Joel prophesied God's promise to pour out His Spirit upon all flesh. God fulfilled His word on the day of Pentecost 2,000 years ago, and is still fulfilling it today.

How do we know this has been fulfilled? Let's go to Acts 1:4-5 and read what Jesus said before He left the Earth. "And, being assembled together with them, *commanded* them that they should not depart from Jerusalem, but wait for *the promise of the Father, which,* saith he [Jesus], *ye have heard of me.* For John truly baptized with water; but *ye shall be baptized with the Holy Ghost* not many days hence" (emphasis added).

Jesus didn't suggest it; but rather, he commanded them to stay in Jerusalem and wait for the Father's promise, where the disciples would be baptized with the Holy Spirit. When He said, "Which ye have heard of me," He was referring to what God had spoken to John the Baptist about Him three years earlier.

In John 1:32-33, John the Baptist prophesied about this upcoming baptism. He said, "I saw the Spirit descending from heaven like a dove, and it abode upon him [Jesus]. And I knew him not: *but he [God] that sent me to baptize with water, the same said unto me,* Upon whom thou shalt see the Spirit descending, and remaining on him, the same is he which *baptizeth with the Holy Ghost.* And I saw, and bare record that this is the Son of God" (emphasis added).

God Himself told John that the man whom the Holy Spirit would descend upon would baptize believers with the Holy Spirit. The prophecy in Joel echoed through the mouth of John the Baptist, but now it contained one more detail. The outpouring of the Spirit promised by the Father in Joel's prophecy would come through the Son of God. According to Jesus' words in Acts 1:5 and Luke 24:49, this promise couldn't be given until His believers waited in Jerusalem.

Mark, Luke, and Matthew also recorded John the Baptist's same words. The Bible says that "in the mouth of two or three witnesses shall every word be established" (2 Cor. 13:1). Four men witnessed and testified this, and Jesus reminded the disciples of this promise in Acts 1:5.

In Acts 1:8, Jesus explained the baptism even further by saying, "But ye shall receive power, after that the Holy Ghost is come upon you: and ye shall be witnesses unto me both in Jerusalem, and in all Judaea, and in Samaria, and unto the uttermost part of the earth." The believers needed this power, or else our Lord would've not commanded them to wait to receive it. They couldn't be witnesses to Him the way the Father intended without this specific baptism.

During His earthly ministry, Jesus also spoke of the Father's promise in great detail in the book of John.

ANOTHER HELPER

On the night of His arrest, Jesus said, "If ye love me, keep my commandments. And I will pray the Father, and he shall give you another Comforter, that he may abide with you for ever" (John 14:15-16). When the disciples heard this, they had been walking with Jesus for three years. Jesus told them that He wouldn't stay with them for much longer, but to their comfort, He assured them that He wouldn't leave them as orphans. He had been their Helper, but another would come to live with them forever.

Jesus said, "Even the Spirit of truth; whom the world cannot receive, because it seeth him not, neither knoweth him: but ye know him; for he dwelleth with you, and shall be in you" (John 14:17). Notice how Jesus specified the

Holy Spirit's role in the disciples' lives at the moment. The Holy Spirit dwelt with the disciples because they believed in the Son of God, but Jesus told them that they needed to receive His infilling.

The world can receive salvation through Jesus Christ; however, the world cannot receive the Holy Spirit's infilling. The baptism with the Holy Spirit is only promised to those who believe in Jesus. For Jesus made it clear: the world will neither be able to recognize nor receive the Holy Spirit unless they put their faith in the Son of God first.

In Luke 11:13, Jesus said, "If you then, being evil, know how to give good gifts to your children, how much more will your heavenly Father give the Holy Spirit to those who ask Him!" Jesus related a father and child relationship on Earth to our relationship with our Father in Heaven. How can a kid walk up to a stranger and ask for something? But when a child runs to their loving father to ask for a gift, the father is overjoyed to give it.

An unbeliever cannot ask for the Holy Spirit unless they are a child of God first. To our great joy, the Word declares, "For ye are all the children of God by faith in Christ Jesus" (Galatians 3:26). If you believe Jesus rose again and confess Him as your Lord, you are a child of

God.

Two Prerequisites

In the book of John, Jesus explicitly referred to a time in the future where those who believed in Him would receive the Holy Spirit. But when would that happen? The Word reveals two events that would happen before the Holy Spirit could come. The Son of God must be glorified and return to sit at the right hand of the Father first.

Jesus Must Be Glorified

John 7:37-39 says, "In the last day, that great day of the feast, Jesus stood and cried, saying, If any man thirst, let him come unto me, and drink. He that believeth on me, as the scripture hath said, out of his belly shall flow rivers of living water. (*But this spake he of the Spirit*, which *they that believe on him should receive*: for the Holy Ghost was *not yet given*; because that *Jesus was not yet glorified*.*) (emphasis added)."

The Holy Spirit would not come until Jesus was glorified—which means His crucifixion and resurrection. We know this because Jesus said, "The hour is come, that the Son of man should be glorified. Verily, verily, I say unto you, Except a corn of wheat fall into the ground and die, it abideth alone: but if it die, it bringeth forth much fruit" (John 12:23-24).

In John 17:1,5, Jesus prayed before he was arrested to be crucified. "Father, the hour is come; glorify thy Son, that thy Son also may glorify thee. . . . And now, O Father, glorify thou me with thine own self with the glory which I had with thee before the world was."

After Jesus detailed the coming of the Holy Spirit to the disciples, Judas Iscariot betrayed him, and the Romans crucified Him because of the Jews' clamor. Three days after His death, the power of God resurrected and glorified Jesus and emptied the tomb. In Hebrews 2:7-8, the author confirmed His glorification. "Thou crownedst him with glory and honour, and didst set him over the works of thy hands: Thou hast put all things in subjection under his feet."

Jesus said, "Before Abraham was, I am" (John 8:58). He is Lord irrespective of time. When He took upon human flesh and walked among us for thirty-three years, He took "upon him the form of a servant" (Phil. 2:7). However once He completed what He came to do, God "highly exalted him, and given him a name which is above every name" (Phil. 2:9).

Jesus Must Return to the Father

In John 16:5-7, Jesus said, "But now I go my way to him [Father] that sent me; and none of you asketh me, Whither goest thou? But because I have said these things unto you, sorrow hath filled your heart. Nevertheless I tell you the truth; It is expedient for you that I go away: for if I go not away, the Comforter will not come unto you; but if I depart, I will send him unto you."

Jesus revealed two things here. First, it's better for us that He returned to the Father and the Holy Spirit could come. If Jesus says it is better, I choose to believe Him. Jesus and the Spirit of God are always in unity; they love us immensely that Jesus said that it's for our benefit.

Second, the coming of the Helper rested upon Jesus leaving the Earth and returning to be with the Father. Jesus needed to leave the Earth so that the Holy Spirit could come and fill those who believed in Him and would believe in Him.

As I've written earlier, the Gospel of John says that after Jesus resurrected, He breathed on the disciples to receive the Holy Spirit. But this was not the baptism with the Holy Spirit, because Jesus' second prerequisite hadn't happened yet. He hadn't yet departed the Earth and sat at the right hand of God.

After Jesus breathed on them to receive the Holy Spirit, He still made it a point to command them to wait for the Father's promise. His commandment reveals that these two events—receiving the Holy Spirit as result of salvation and receiving Jesus' baptism—were separate from one another. So, after leaving His final instructions, He left the Earth to sit at the Father's right hand (Mark 16:19, 1 Peter 3:22).

What God had spoken through Joel hundreds of years before the disciples' births was nearing its naissance. So, the believers obeyed—all one hundred and twenty of them. In a room in Jerusalem, the eleven disciples and Matthias, Jesus' mother Mary, His siblings, and about a hundred more believers gathered. In faith, they waited with great anticipation.

3

FULFILLMENT OF THE PROMISE

> "The grace of the Lord Jesus Christ, and
> the love of God, and the communion of
> the Holy Spirit be with you all."
>
> — 2 CORINTHIANS 13:14

A S THE BELIEVERS WAITED PRAYERFULLY, THE FEAST of Pentecost approached. At the time, Jews from all over the world migrated to Jerusalem to celebrate. Jesus had left with a promise to return one day, but until then, His believers needed to receive another Helper to be with them on Earth.

One morning, Jesus decided to pour Him out. Acts 2:1-4 says, "And when the day of Pentecost was fully come, they were all with one accord in one place. And suddenly there came a sound from heaven as of a rushing mighty wind, and it filled all the house where they were sitting.

And there appeared unto them cloven tongues like as of fire, and it sat upon each of them. And they were all filled with the Holy Ghost, and began to speak with other tongues, as the Spirit gave them utterance."

The Father gave Jesus the Holy Spirit to pour out and Jesus fulfilled His word by filling each of the one hundred and twenty believers with the Holy Spirit. As a result, they began to speak in different languages. It was the Holy Spirit whom Jesus promised who gave them the ability to speak in other languages.

In Mark 16:15-18, Jesus spoke of believers speaking in new languages when He gave the Great Commission. "Go ye into all the world, and preach the gospel to every creature. He that believeth and is baptized shall be saved; but he that believeth not shall be damned. And these signs shall follow them that believe; In my name shall they cast out devils; they shall speak with new tongues; They shall take up serpents; and if they drink any deadly thing, it shall not hurt them; they shall lay hands on the sick, and they shall recover."

When speaking to the disciples, Jesus said, "In my name shall *they* cast out devils; *they* shall speak with new tongues" (emphasis added). He didn't tell the disciples, "In my name

shall *you* cast out devils; *you* shall speak with new tongues."
He was speaking of the signs that would follow the men
and women who would believe the gospel *as a result* of the
disciples' preaching. Even today, we are the fruits of the
eleven disciples obeying God and preaching the gospel.

According to Jesus' words, speaking in new tongues
or languages is a sign that will follow a believer. So, as a
result of Jesus pouring out the Holy Spirit on the believers
in Jerusalem, they began to speak in new tongues. The
international Jews heard them speak in different languages
and actually understood them. Acts 2:7–8,11 says, "And
they were all amazed and marvelled, saying one to another,
Behold, are not all these which speak Galilaeans? And how
hear we every man in our own tongue, wherein we were
born? . . . Cretes and Arabians, we do hear them speak
in our tongues the wonderful works of God."

The visiting Jews heard these simple men and women
speaking of God's marvelous works in their own languages.
The Spirit had given the believers the ability to speak about
God in languages they didn't naturally know how to speak.

How did these visitors react to this? Acts 2:12-13 says,
"And they were all amazed, and were in doubt, saying one
to another, What meaneth this? Others mocking said,

These men are full of new wine."

When Peter heard this, he stood up with the Eleven, and clarified what was happening. "For these are not drunken, as ye suppose, seeing it is but the third hour of the day. *But this is that which was spoken by the prophet Joel*" (Acts 2:15-16).

Remember the prophecy in Joel? The Holy Spirit revealed to Peter that the Holy Spirit being poured out on their lives was the fulfillment of Joel's prophecy told long ago. Then Peter cited what God said through the prophet Joel and proceeded to preach the gospel to the international Jews. Then towards the end of his sermon, he explained why they were all speaking in other languages.

"This Jesus hath God raised up, whereof we all are witnesses. Therefore being by the right hand of God exalted, and *having received of the Father the promise of the Holy Ghost*, he hath shed forth this, *which ye now see and hear*" (Acts 2:32-33; emphasis added). The Father gave the promise of the Holy Spirit to Jesus to pour out upon believers. The transfer could only happen if Jesus departed the Earth and sat at the right hand of God.

It was neither the Father nor the Holy Spirit who baptized the believers. It was Jesus Himself who baptized them from His seat in Heaven; *He* is the one who holds the promise of the Holy Spirit.

When the Holy Spirit is poured upon someone, a manifestation occurs that one can both *see* and *hear*. It's an event that is witnessed by a person's physical senses. The Jews both saw and heard them. And when some said they were drunk, Peter explained in other words, "No, we are not drunk. This is God's promise in Joel to pour out His Spirit."

After thousands of Jews heard Peter preach the gospel, they were convicted and asked him what they should do.

Peter replied, "Repent, and let every one of you be baptized in the name of Jesus Christ for the remission of sins; and *you shall receive the gift of the Holy Spirit. For the promise* is to you and to your children, and to all who are afar off, as many as the Lord our God will call" (Acts 2:38-39; emphasis added).

Peter laid it out for them by telling them to turn away from their sins and be baptized in the name of Jesus. Then they would receive the Father's promise. So, like the Samaritans in Acts 8, after they believed and got baptized in water, they still needed to receive the gift of the Holy Spirit.

A few chapters down, when Peter and the apostles were brought forth to the Sanhedrin and interrogated by the high priest, they told them, "Him [Jesus] hath God exalted with his right hand to be a prince and a Saviour, for to give repentance to Israel, and forgiveness of sins. And we are His witnesses of these things; and *so is also the Holy Ghost, whom God hath given to them that obey him*" (Acts 5:29-32; emphasis added). The Holy Spirit is given to those who obey God! He is not given to the world; He is poured out upon those who become God's children.

To *All* Who Are Far Off

In Acts 2:39, Peter said, "For the promise is unto you, and to your children, and to all that are afar off, even as many as the Lord our God shall call." He told the thousands listening to him that the same gift he received—the Holy Spirit and speaking in tongues—was for them and their children.

Three thousand people repented after Peter preached. So, let's add 3,000 more people to represent their children. With roughly 6,000 people in mind, Peter went even further and said that the gift is to *all* who are far off and as many as the Lord will call.

That's a number like the sand of the sea; men would give up counting. Their children would teach their children of the promise of the Father or in other words, the baptism with the Holy Spirit. If God would have declared for this wonder and gift to cease after a certain number of years, Peter would've not uttered that sentence. Instead he revealed the plan of God; this promise was for all future generations.

Today, many people believe in the gospel and partake in the biblical ordinance of water baptism and believe they possess the complete foundation for their faith journey on Earth. However, the 120 believers, the 3,000 believers on the day of Pentecost, and the Samaritan believers did not walk on the complete foundation they needed—at least not until they were baptized with the Holy Spirit by Jesus Christ.

4

THE SIGN

"For by one Spirit are we all baptized into
one body, whether we be Jews or Gentiles,
whether we be bond or free; and have
been all made to drink into one Spirit."

— I Corinthians 12:13

WHEN THE 120 BELIEVERS RECEIVED THE BAPTISM with the Holy Spirit and spoke in tongues on the day of Pentecost, they assumed that God had given that gift only to the Jewish race. However, ten years after that day, they came to the revelation that the marvelous experience was for the Gentiles as well.

Acts 10 and 11 contains the story of Peter and a centurion named Cornelius. This centurion wasn't a Jew, but a Gentile or another word for a non-Jew. Back then, Jews refused to associate with Gentiles, for their many dietary laws made them fearful of eating at a Gentile's home and thus, disobeying God by eating something unclean. Along with other laws such as forbidding intermarriage, most Jews avoided communion with the Gentiles altogether.

Through divine actions, God orchestrated a meeting between Cornelius and Peter. He led Peter to Cornelius' house to preach the gospel to him, and in preparation, Cornelius had gathered his relatives and close friends. When Peter arrived, Cornelius told him they were all ready to hear everything God commanded him to speak.

Peter began to preach the gospel to them, and when he arrived at Jesus' resurrection and forgiveness of sins, something sudden happened. Acts 10:44 says, "While Peter yet spake these words, the Holy Ghost fell on all them which heard the word." Peter did not ask nor lay hands for them to receive Him; the Holy Spirit came as faith generated in their hearts from hearing the Word of God.

"And they of the circumcision which believed were *astonished*, as many as came with Peter, because that on the Gentiles *also* was poured out *the gift of the Holy Ghost*. For they heard them *speak with tongues, and magnify God*" (Acts 10:45-46; emphasis added).

In this context, the people of the circumcision were

believers who happened to be Jewish. They had accompanied Peter to this centurion's house and marveled at the sight before them. God had poured out the same gift they received on the day of Pentecost on the Gentiles.

How did the Jews *know* the Gentiles received the Holy Spirit? The Bible says, "*For* they heard them speak with tongues, and magnify God." According to Strong's Concordance, the Greek word used for "for" is *gar* which means, "A primary particle; properly, assigning a reason." What was the reason they knew the Gentiles received the gift of the Holy Spirit? They heard them speak in tongues and exalt the Lord.

If nothing happened, how could they have known that the Gentiles received the Holy Spirit? God gave us a physical sign that we can "see and hear," as Peter said in Acts 2, to know. That was how the Jews knew the Gentiles received the infilling of the Holy Spirit: the same thing happened to them in Acts 2.

If we place these two outpourings of the Spirit side by side, we can see the parallels. On the day of Pentecost, the Christian Jews received the Holy Spirit and spoke in tongues and magnified God. Afterwards, they were "astonished," because with their own eyes and ears, they witnessed the same event happen with the Gentiles at Cornelius' house.

When they witnessed and heard them speak in tongues and magnify God, it sealed the deal for them. The gospel wasn't just for them, but for the whole world as well. Did they forget Jesus' words before He left the Earth? "But ye shall receive power, after that the Holy Ghost is come upon you: and ye shall be witnesses unto me both in Jerusalem, and in all Judaea, and in Samaria, and unto *the uttermost part of the earth*" (Acts 1:8; emphasis added).

GOD GAVE THEM THE SAME GIFT

After that experience at Cornelius' house, Peter returned to Jerusalem and testified to the apostles about what had happened.

"And as I began to speak, *the Holy Ghost fell on them, as on us at the beginning.* Then remembered I the word of the Lord, how that he said, John indeed baptized with water; *but ye shall be baptized with the Holy Ghost.* Forasmuch then as *God gave them the like gift as he did unto us*, who believed on the Lord Jesus Christ; what was I, that I could withstand God?" (Acts 11:15-17; emphasis added).

Peter remembered what Jesus promised them in Acts

1. How did he know Cornelius and his guests received the Holy Spirit? He compared it to the day of Pentecost and declared that they received the same gift he and the apostles received. They all began to speak in other languages and declare God's greatness.

Simon Sees

Let's return to Acts 8 and go further into the story of when a newly-converted man named Simon tried to *buy* the Holy Spirit from Peter. When we visited this biblical chapter in the first chapter of this book, we had read how Philip had gone to a city in Samaria to preach the gospel. After the apostles in Jerusalem heard that men and women had given their lives to Christ, they sent Peter and John to them so that the new believers might receive the Holy Spirit.

One of those converts, a man named Simon, watched people receive the baptism with the Holy Spirit. Acts 8:18-19 says, "And when Simon saw that through laying on of the apostles' hands the Holy Ghost was given, he offered them money, Saying, Give me also this power, that on whomsoever I lay hands, he may receive the Holy Ghost."

Note the words, "When Simon *saw* . . ." (Acts 8:18; emphasis added). The Spirit of God cannot be seen for He is invisible. For Simon to *see*, there must have been some sort of physical manifestation for him to see the Spirit of God poured out on the believers.

Some may argue and say, "Oh, they could have been filled with joy." The Bible says the people were filled with joy when God manifested miracles and deliverance through Phillip in Samaria in Acts 8:8. Yet Peter and John still had to come down to pray for the believers so they might receive the Holy Spirit. So, it must have been another physical manifestation that Simon must have seen. Could it have been speaking in tongues and declaring God's greatness?

THE TWELVE DISCIPLES

In Acts 19, Paul came across twelve disciples in Ephesus and asked them if they received the Holy Spirit when they believed. Surprisingly, they hadn't even heard of the Holy Spirit and revealed that they had only been baptized with John's baptism. Paul realized and told them that they hadn't even been baptized in the water in the name of Jesus; they were only baptized by John the Baptist.

Acts 19:5-6 says, "When they [the twelve disciples] heard this, they were baptized in the name of the Lord

Jesus. And when Paul had laid his hands upon them, the Holy Ghost came on them; and they spake with tongues, and prophesied."

So first, these disciples were baptized in the water in the name of Jesus, and then Paul prayed for them to receive the Holy Spirit. As a result, the men received the baptism with the Holy Spirit and began to speak in tongues.

If Paul had prayed for the twelve disciples to receive the Holy Spirit, this implies that he had also received Him. Paul wasn't present on the day of Pentecost and didn't receive it from an apostle laying hands on him. Instead, he received Him through the prayers of an ordinary believer.

ANANIAS

Before Paul was saved, he persecuted Christians violently. Acts 9:1 details that he breathed "threatenings and slaughter against the disciples of the Lord." He sought to discover believers so he could throw them in jail and even watched the coats of those who stoned Stephen, the first martyr.

One day, God appeared to him through a bright light and spoke to him. As a result, Paul became blind and so, his companions brought him into a city called Damascus where Paul did not eat or drink for three days and nights.

A disciple named Ananias lived in the same city. The Bible does not call him an apostle or a prophet—only a disciple. The Lord spoke to him to go to Paul and pray for him. Ananias obeyed and went. When he arrived to where Paul was staying, he told him, "Brother Saul [Paul], *the Lord, even Jesus,* that appeared unto thee in the way as thou camest, *hath sent me,* that thou mightest receive thy sight, and *be filled with the Holy Ghost*" (Acts 9:17; emphasis added).

No man sent Ananias, unlike the story of Samaria where the apostles in Jerusalem sent Peter and John. God appeared to Ananias in a vision to pray for Paul to be filled with the Holy Spirit.

God didn't choose any of the original eleven disciples to pray for Paul to be filled with the Holy Spirit. He chose a believer in Damascus. If God chose a disciple like Ananias, how can we possibly withstand God? He chooses and directs any believer He wishes to pray for another believer to receive His Spirit.

Acts 9:18 says, "And immediately there fell from his [Paul's] eyes as it had been scales: and he received sight forthwith, and arose, and was baptized." Now, it doesn't say here that Paul spoke in tongues, but in 1 Corinthians 14:18, he confessed it in a letter, "I thank my God, I speak with tongues more than ye all."

Through these five stories, the Word reveals that speaking in tongues and magnifying God is the evidential sign that a believer has received the baptism with the Holy Spirit. We see it implied in the story of Simon attempting to buy it, but it is clear as day in the records of the day of Pentecost, Cornelius' and his relatives' and friends' lives, the twelve disciples Paul prayed for, and Paul's own life.

If through the mouth of two or three witnesses a fact can be established, then how about four concrete records? We have the Holy Spirit because we are saved, for those who are led by the Spirit of God are sons of God. However, Jesus' commandment is for us to receive His baptism, where He baptizes us with the Holy Spirit. And the sign which we both "can see and hear" is speaking in tongues.

If our Lord said we would speak in tongues, I venture to write that therein lies a great significance. Salvation trumps this importance of course; a believer can go to Heaven never receiving the outpouring of the Holy Spirit and speaking in tongues. However, the beauty of eternal life does not dissipate our Lord's commandments for our earthly life. The Father promised it because it is worthy in a believer's journey.

5

THE GREAT SIGNIFICANCE

"For he that speaketh in an unknown
tongue speaketh not unto men, but unto
God."

— 1 CORINTHIANS 14:2

RECEIVING JESUS' BAPTISM WAS AN EVENT OF GREAT urgency in the early church and still should be today. Rooted in the Word of God, the significance of our Father's promise has remained the same despite the modern-day church's embrace, indifference, or rejection of it. God thoroughly expresses its importance through His promises in the Bible and actions in the book of Acts. For example, in the lives of the 120 believers and Cornelius and his guests, Jesus poured out the Holy Spirit with no human hand laying upon them. Later on, it was

He who told Ananias to pray for a newly-converted Paul to be filled with the Holy Spirit.

The early church followed in Jesus' footsteps and knew it was the Father's will for every believer to receive Him. Peter declared that the gift was for the 3,000 men and women listening to him and their children and all who were far off. It carried such value that the Jerusalem apostles sent Peter and John to the new believers in Samaria to pray for them to receive Him. And Paul made sure to inquire the twelve believers in Ephesus if they had received Him.

Acts 6 details that a multitude of men and women came to the faith. During this time a problem arose as some complained that the widows weren't being fed. So, the Twelve who had walked with Jesus on Earth told the multitude to search for seven men to take up the duty to feed the widows.

They listed three qualities to look for in each man. Each man had to be of honest report and *full of the Holy Spirit* and wisdom. Among the multitude, they found Philip, Stephen, Prochorus, Nicanor, Timon, and Parmenas. Acts 11:24 also describes a different man named Barnabas, who had worked together with Paul, as a "good man, and full of the Holy Ghost and of faith" who brought many people to the Lord.

What is a sign that someone is filled with the Holy Spirit? On the day of Pentecost, the believers spoke in tongues as a result of being filled with the Holy Spirit. Acts 2:4 says, "And they were all filled with the Holy Ghost, and began to speak with other tongues, as the Spirit gave them utterance."

If the Holy Spirit through Peter said all believers could receive this gift, the same goes for these seven men and Barnabas. And if tongues is given to an individual who has become filled with the Spirit, then these men spoke in tongues as well. When Paul declared, "I thank my God, I speak with tongues more than ye all," there were also some, if not all, in the Corinthian church who had received the Holy Spirit and spoke in tongues (1 Cor. 14:18).

SPEAKING TO GOD

First Corinthians 14:1 says that when we speak in a new language, we speak to God and no one else. This fact should be forefront in our minds when we speak in tongues. We are not unleashing empty words into the air, but a Spirit-given language to speak to God. When we pray in tongues, we collaborate with the Holy Spirit for He gives our spirits the words to speak in the new language. "No man understandeth him; howbeit in the spirit he speaketh mysteries" (1 Cor. 14:2). No one understands us, including ourselves (unless the Lord provides the interpretation).

When we pray in tongues, it is our *spirits*, not our souls, who pray. "For if I pray in an unknown tongue, *my spirit prayeth*, but my understanding is unfruitful. What is it then? *I will pray with the spirit*, and I will pray with the understanding also: *I will sing with the spirit*, and I will sing with the understanding also" (1 Cor. 14:14-15; emphasis added).

We should pray with their understanding *and* spirit. You may ask, "Well, how do I know what I am praying?" Perhaps God wants us to pray things that if we knew what we prayed for, our pride would resist and we'd refuse to utter the words. Trust the Lord for it is an act of faith. God Himself will give your spirit the right words to pray (Acts 2:4).

The Bible reveals that as prophecy edifies the church, speaking in an unknown tongue edifies the believer (1 Cor. 14:4). Webster's 1828 Dictionary defines edification as "a building up, in a moral and religious sense; instruction; improvement and progress of the mind, in knowledge, in morals, or in faith and holiness." God gives a believer a new language to improve them in a spiritual sense. Why do you think Paul wrote that he spoke in tongues more than all the people at the Corinthian church? He understood the importance of it and his need to be edified and made it a habit in his life.

Despite his great calling from God and extraordinary life, Paul was human like us. He said, "We also are men of like passions with you, and preach unto you that ye should turn from these vanities unto the living God" (Acts 14:15). If it didn't make a difference in his life, Paul neither wouldn't have done it nor instructed it for the church to do it as well (1 Cor. 14:5).

Throughout our lives, we will always need to improve ourselves. The Word tells us to pray always in the Spirit, so speaking in tongues should be a daily habit. We are praying for ourselves so that we may improve as a person of faith. The closer we get to God and become more like Him, we love Him and others more.

Jude wrote, "But ye, beloved, *building up yourselves* on your most holy faith, *praying in the Holy Ghost*" (Jude 1:20; emphasis added). How do you build or edify yourself in your most holy faith? By praying in the Spirit, which is praying in tongues.

You can pray for yourself and pray for saints or fellow Christians in tongues as well. Ephesians 6:18 says, "*Praying* always with all prayer and supplication *in the Spirit*, and watching thereunto with all perseverance and supplication *for all saints*" (emphasis added). Paul instructed the church to pray in the Spirit for all saints. If you don't know how to pray for someone, pray in the Spirit for He knows the right words to pray.

PROPHECY AND TONGUES

Above all, Paul recognized that understandable words should be spoken in the church. Tongues edifies the one who speaks it, except for when the Holy Spirit gives the interpretation through a believer. The baptism and tongues should be taught from the pulpit; however, one should be sensitive to speaking in tongues from the pulpit. Paul declared that it is better to speak with your understanding so that others may be edified. Why? All things should be done in love.

This is why the first thing Paul wrote at the beginning of 1 Corinthians 14 is, "Follow after charity, and desire spiritual gifts, but rather that ye may prophesy." Pursue charity or in other words, pursue *love* in the church. When you are speaking in tongues in the pulpit, you are not edifying anyone but yourself (unless you are praying for a fellow believer in the Spirit). But rather, seek to prophesy so that you may encourage and instruct the church.

Acts 2, 10, and 19 reveal three events where multiple people spoke in tongues in a group setting. In these three chapters, the Bible shows that there is nothing wrong with praying in tongues together. All of the believers had received the baptism and prayed in tongues at the same time.

All in all, Paul concluded the matter in the following verses. "Wherefore, brethren, covet to prophesy, and forbid not to speak with tongues. Let all things be done decently and in order" (1 Cor. 14:39-40). Love, decency, and order should be our guideposts when we come together to worship the Lord.

THE GIFTS OF THE SPIRIT

Some people have confused the baptism with the Holy Spirit with the gifts of the Holy Spirit, when they are different from one another. First Corinthians 12 defines the purpose of the gifts of the Spirit differently from the language which comes from the baptism with the Spirit.

"Now there are diversities of gifts, but the same Spirit.

…But the manifestation of the Spirit is given to every man to *profit withal*. For to one is given by the Spirit the word of wisdom; to another the word of knowledge by the same Spirit … *to another divers kinds of tongues; to another the interpretation of tongues:* But all these worketh that one and the selfsame Spirit, *dividing to every man* severally *as he will*" (1 Cor. 12:4,7-8,10-11; emphasis added).

The Holy Spirit distributes and manifests His gifts to each believer as He wills. A believer can receive the gifts of healing, while another can receive the gift of the word of knowledge. The Bible also tells us to be zealous after spiritual gifts, so we can desire them earnestly. The Lord can give more than one or all gifts to an individual. It's as He wills combined with our pursuit of them!

"But the manifestation of the Spirit is given to every man to profit withal" (1 Cor. 12:7). When the Holy Spirit manifests the gifts of diverse kinds of tongues and interpretation, He, *not* the believer, initiates the specific tongue and then gives the interpretation either to the same person or another. The purpose of the gifts is to benefit the church rather than the individual only.

On the other hand, the unknown tongue (which comes from the baptism with the Holy Spirit) is to edify the individual. First Corinthians 14:4 says, "He that speaketh in an unknown tongue edifieth himself." The baptism with the Holy Spirit allows the believer to speak in tongues anytime they wish and for as long as they desire. They don't wait on a *manifestation* of the Spirit to pray in tongues, for the language they received is the one which edifies themselves.

My spirit is under my control. When I decide, my spirit prays and as a result, I speak in tongues. This is why Paul wrote, "Yet in the church *I* had rather speak five words with my understanding, that by my voice I might teach others also, than ten thousand words in an unknown tongue" (1 Cor. 14:19; emphasis added). Paul could speak ten thousand words in an unknown tongue if he was willing, but out of love for the church, he'd rather speak with his understanding.

At any point, the Holy Spirit could've interrupted one of Paul's sermons and given him the gift of diverse tongues to speak a message out to the church, and then also given him or someone else the interpretation. This also could've been a known language a person from another country could've understood, but that Paul didn't know how to speak. Only then Paul would step into the gift of diverse kinds of tongues because of the manifestation of the Spirit.

It is as the Spirit wills. We must be yielded to Him at all times. He knows what benefits the church at any certain time.

First Corinthians 12:28-31 says, "And God hath set some in the church, first apostles, secondarily prophets, thirdly teachers, after that miracles, then gifts of healings, helps, governments, *diversities of tongues*. Are all apostles? are all prophets? are all teachers? are all workers of miracles? Have all the gifts of healing? *do all speak with tongues? do all interpret?* But covet earnestly the best gifts…" (emphasis added).

God has called some of His children to different types of ministries. Some men and women are given the gifts of healings. In Mark 16, we read that all believers can pray for healing for others, but God calls specific people to dedicate themselves to that area and steward a ministry of healing.

For example, when God calls a person to be a teacher of the Word in the church, this doesn't mean a person without that calling can never teach the Word. The person simply isn't called to lead a teaching ministry. Teachers devote their lives studying the Word and improving their skills for the glory of God. It is the specific calling He has called them to enter, and they spend their lives teaching others.

All in all, the purpose of the gifts is to profit the church, while the tongue or language a believer receives is to edify themselves and to be used as a fantastic way to pray for others. Remember that when we are speaking in tongues, we are praying to God. Like arrows, our prayers pierce past the heavens and reaches God's ears.

We must build up ourselves in the faith and speaking in tongues is one of the key ways. It is not a matter of preference or opinion, but rather obedience to the Word of God. It is a powerful and humbling act of yielding to God and trusting Him.

ONE ACCORD

Everything the men of God wrote in the New Testament letters is based on the salvation of Jesus Christ in the Gospels and the fulfillment of Jesus' baptism with the Holy Spirit upon believers in Acts. Many churches stop at the salvation of the spirit and water baptism and then attempt to understand what the letters say of the Holy Spirit. As a result, many people receive a limited view of

Him and His role in their lives.

It is impossible to fully understand everything written in the New Testament letters about the Holy Spirit unless we understand what the *entire* Bible speaks of Him. We must ask: why was it more important for Him to come and Jesus to go? What is His role here on Earth? Why is it necessary for Him to fill us and give us His power? If He is called our Helper, then in what areas of our lives did He come to help us?

We must seek the answers out in the Bible. In the next chapter, we shall scratch the surface of the wonderfulness of the person: the Holy Spirit.

6

OUR HELPER

"Forasmuch as ye are manifestly declared
to be the epistle of Christ ministered by us,
written not with ink, but with the Spirit
of the living God; not in tables of stone,
but in fleshy tables of the heart."

— 2 CORINTHIANS 3:3

WHEN WE RECEIVE JESUS' OUTPOURING OF THE Holy Spirit, we receive Him as our Helper. As we will read in Jesus' description of the Holy Spirit, the matter of receiving the following benefits of Him is dependent upon us receiving Him like Cornelius or the believers of Samaria. And as one of the prerequisites for His coming, Jesus said, "If I go not away, the Comforter will not come unto you; but if I depart, I will send him unto you" (John 16:7).

After Jesus came to Earth, accomplished His mission, and ascended, the Holy Spirit came down to accomplish His role. It is *His* time now to work in our lives on Earth, and one of His great purposes is to point to Jesus. It is impossible to fully walk into everything our Father has for us unless we first receive the Helper.

There are many facets to the Holy Spirit, and in order to know someone better—or in this case, God Himself—we must seek what the Word says about Him. One thing we must stand convicted of is that He possesses great power, but He is not *a* power. He is one of the three of the godhead: the Father, Jesus Christ, and the Holy Spirit. Jesus defended His work so much so that He declared that blasphemy against Him would never be forgiven.

The Holy Spirit loves to teach, reveal, and guide us. He is the wondrous, patient, and loving Spirit of God, who glorifies Jesus Christ and works miracles in our lives. However, we should not pursue Him for His benefits, we should desire Him because He is God. We should love Him because He first loved us.

OUR MARVELOUS PARACLETE

In the Greek language, Jesus calls the Holy Spirit our *paraklétos* or in English, our paraclete. According to Webster's 1828 Dictionary, a paraclete is "properly, an advocate; one called to aid or support; hence, the consoler, comforter or intercessor, a term applied to the Holy Spirit." This is an all-in-one term for Him.

The Spirit helps us in our weaknesses and when we do not pray as we should, He intercedes for us according to God's will (Rom. 8:26). Jesus intercedes for us at the right hand of God, while the Holy Spirit intercedes for us so deeply that words do not come out. How great and overwhelming is the love of God for us!

Whatever our weaknesses may be, He desires to help us in them. We need His help to avoid bowing down to sin; He strengthens us for the glory of Jesus. This is why Paul prayed in Ephesians 3:16, asking the Father that the believers would "be strengthened with might by his Spirit in the inner man." How do we become strengthened? By God's Spirit.

THE SPIRIT OF TRUTH

In John 15:26, Jesus said, "But when the Comforter is

come, whom I will send unto you from the Father, even the Spirit of truth, which proceedeth from the Father, he shall testify of me." In a world full of lies, deceit, and doctrines of demons, we need the Spirit of truth to guide and counsel us along with the Scriptures. We must be people of the Word *and* the Spirit.

When praying to the Father, Jesus said, "Sanctify them through thy truth: thy word is truth" (John 17:17). Paul wrote that the sword of the Spirit is the word of God. The Spirit of God and the Word will never contradict each other. The Holy Spirit wrote the Bible through men; what better way to understand the Scriptures than to learn directly from the One who authored it?

The same Holy Spirit who authored the Scriptures also teaches believers all things. Jesus said, "He [the Holy Spirit] shall teach you all things, and bring all things to your remembrance, whatsoever I have said unto you" (John 14:26). The Spirit of truth longs to teach you His Word and will reveal deep things of the Word to you as you read it. You cannot understand the Word without Him.

Paul wrote, "Now we have received, not the spirit of the world, but the spirit which is of God; *that we might know the things that are freely given to us of God*. Which things also we speak, not in words which man's wisdom teacheth, but *which the Holy Ghost teacheth"* (1 Cor. 2:12-13; emphasis added). Paul deemed the Holy Spirit's teachings more important than the teachings he received from intelligent mentors and declared that the words he spoke were taught by Him.

In the same way, the Holy Spirit longs to teach us. God has given us things that we cannot know or understand without receiving the Spirit first. He is the condition for us to know the full riches of God's provision for us.

Jesus said, "And when they bring you unto the synagogues, and unto magistrates, and powers, take ye no thought how or what thing ye shall answer, or what ye shall say: For *the Holy Ghost shall teach you* in the same hour what ye ought to say" (Luke 12:11-12; emphasis added). In the book of Acts, we see Jesus' words come to life in Stephen before he was martyred, and when Peter, John, and Paul were taken before authorities. When we receive the Holy Spirit, He will teach us what to say, especially in difficult and persecuting times.

HE SHALL SPEAK WHAT HE HEARS

In John 16:13, Jesus said, "Howbeit when he, the Spirit

of truth, is come, he will guide you into all truth: for he shall not speak of himself; but whatsoever he shall hear, that shall he speak . . ."

As Jesus did not speak on His own authority while He was on Earth, the Holy Spirit will not speak on His own authority while He is on Earth. So whenever the Holy Spirit speaks, He will speak only what He hears.

When Philip saw an Ethiopian eunuch riding in a chariot, the Spirit directed Philip with these words: "Go near, and join thyself to this chariot" (Acts 8:29). As a result, Phillip preached the gospel to him, and the eunuch believed in Jesus. Here we see one of the first recorded signs of the Holy Spirit speaking to believers after He had come upon them.

Another recorded moment is in Acts 13:2. "As they ministered to the Lord, and fasted, the Holy Ghost said, Separate me Barnabas and Saul for the work whereunto I have called them." Paul also declared in Acts 20:23, "Save that the Holy Ghost witnesseth in every city, saying that bonds and afflictions abide me."

When Peter had the vision of the unclean animals in the sky, the Spirit told him, "Behold, three men seek thee. Arise therefore, and get thee down, and go with them, doubting nothing: for I have sent them" (Acts 10:19-20). Peter did not know that three men were seeking him, but the Holy Spirit told him before he encountered them.

Now, let's go back to *before* the Holy Spirit came upon the disciples. Judas Iscariot was dead and the disciples desired to find his replacement. Keep in mind, they were saved, but hadn't yet received Jesus' baptism. In Acts 1, they found two men who had been with Jesus since John's baptism. Instead of the Holy Spirit speaking to them, the believers cast lots and on whoever the object landed, that person would take the vacant spot.

Now, the Bible doesn't record another instance of the believers casting lots *after* receiving the baptism with the Holy Spirit, because when they received Him, they received the Spirit of truth who will guide them and instruct them what to do.

Just like the Holy Spirit spoke to the believers in the book of Acts, He earnestly desires to speak to us. We must learn to listen as He longs to direct us as He did the early church. He desires to speak directly to you and about your situation, just as He did for Peter, Paul, and Barnabas.

SONS AND DAUGHTERS SHALL PROPHESY

When we read Joel 2, the condition upon which men and women would prophesy is when the Holy Spirit is poured out on them. We see this fulfilled when Paul prayed for the twelve disciples to receive the Holy Spirit. Acts 19:6 says, "And when Paul had laid his hands upon them, the Holy Ghost came on them; and they spake with tongues, and *prophesied*" (emphasis added). When Paul went to Phillip's house, he saw Phillip's four daughters who all prophesied. Their ability to prophesy reveals they had all received the baptism with the Holy Spirit.

Jesus said, ". . . and he [the Holy Spirit] will shew [show] you things to come" (John 16:13). Acts 21:11 tells us of a prophet named Agabus who received a message from the Holy Spirit regarding Paul's life. "And when he [Agabus] was come unto us, he took Paul's girdle, and bound his own hands and feet, and said, Thus saith the Holy Ghost, So shall the Jews at Jerusalem bind the man that owneth this girdle, and shall deliver him into the hands of the Gentiles."

The Holy Spirit revealed through Agabus that Paul would be arrested if he went to Jerusalem, and it happened exactly as he prophesied. In another instance, the Lord spoke to Ananias about His plan for Paul's life. "But the Lord said unto him [Ananias], Go thy way: for he [Paul] is a chosen vessel unto me, to bear my name before the Gentiles, and kings, and the children of Israel: For I will shew him how great things he must suffer for my name's sake" (Acts 9:15-16).

As we read in the book of Acts and the letters, Paul suffered and was imprisoned for Christ, and everything else the Lord had spoken about him had come true. In Acts 11, the Holy Spirit spoke through a man by the same name of Agabus that there would come a great famine, and it happened as He said. As a result, all the disciples sent relief to those who were about to go through the famine in Judea.

In 1 Corinthians 14, Paul wrote that God gave prophecy to edify, exhort, and comfort the church. When we edify, we are instructing the church in order to build them up and aid them in their walk with Christ. Webster's 1828 Dictionary defines exhortation as "the form of words intended to incite and encourage" and "advice; counsel." Lastly, comfort is "to strengthen; to invigorate; to cheer or enliven."

As we read above in Joel 2 and Acts 2, God declared that He would pour out His Spirit on all flesh and that sons and daughters would prophesy. Men and women are called to prophesy, and thus, through prophecy, they can instruct, encourage, and invigorate the church.

VISIONS AND DREAMS

In Joel, God also promised that when He pours out His Spirit that we shall see visions and dream dreams. The Lord uses visions and dreams to direct His children and speak to them. We see this in the story of Peter in his vision of the unclean animals when God told him to kill and eat.

In Acts 18, the Lord spoke to Paul through a vision to not be afraid. And in Acts 22, Paul himself declared that he was in a trance and saw the Lord speak to him to leave Jerusalem quickly. Ananias received a vision from the Lord to pray for Paul to be healed and filled with the Spirit. The book of Revelation also contains visions John received from Him.

God is not a respecter of persons; He gives visions to whom He wishes. There is no record of believers seeking visions or dreams, so I do not recommend we seek visions and dreams out. We must keep our eyes on Jesus and a believing heart in the promises of God—that what He said, He will do. He promises that we will have visions and dream dreams according to His power and will. The Spirit will do it when He wants—not when we want!

GLORIFIER OF JESUS CHRIST

The Holy Spirit will always glorify Jesus! Whenever He is present, be assured that the person and name of Jesus will be glorified. The Holy Spirit doesn't point at Himself, but always points to Jesus. He takes from what belongs to Jesus' and declares it to us. He directs our devotion and worship to the Son of God.

We know this because Jesus said, "He [the Holy Spirit] shall glorify me: for he shall receive of mine, and shall shew it unto you. All things that the Father hath are mine: therefore said I, that he shall take of mine, and shall shew it unto you" (John 16:14-15).

When Stephen was about to die, the Bible described a wonderful moment. "But he, *being full of the Holy Ghost*, looked up stedfastly into heaven, and *saw the glory of God, and Jesus standing on the right hand of God*, And said, "Behold, I see the heavens opened, and the Son of man standing on the right hand of God" (Acts 7:55-56; emphasis added).

Note carefully how Stephen was full of the Holy Spirit and *then* saw Jesus standing at the right hand of God.

Whenever the Holy Spirit moves, He will always exalt Jesus Christ, for it is by Jesus that we are saved. He will never glorify angels or people.

POWER OF GOD

Jesus promised that when the Holy Spirit comes upon us, we will receive power and be witnesses to Him. If the disciples needed it even after spending three years with the Lord, we need it as well. We need this power to be witnesses to Jesus, cast out demons, and pray for the sick.

CAST OUT EVIL SPIRITS

In Matthew 12:28, Jesus revealed, "But if I cast out devils by the Spirit of God, then the kingdom of God is come unto you." Jesus' name releases the Holy Spirit's power to expel demons and destroy demonic strongholds over people. How we need His power to see ourselves and others free! The expulsion of demons in people's lives is a sign of God's kingdom coming to Earth. According to Jesus' words, when we pray "thy kingdom come," which is in the Lord's Prayer, we are also praying for freedom from demonic oppression over people's lives.

Before Jesus joined our heavenly Father, He said that one of the signs of those who believe in Him is the casting out of evil spirits. "And these signs shall follow them that believe; In my name shall they cast out devils" (Mark 16:17). In Ephesians 6:12, Paul emphasized that *our* battle is not "against flesh and blood, but against principalities, against powers, against the rulers of the darkness of this world, against spiritual wickedness in high places."

When Phillip went to Samaria to preach the gospel, he cast out evil spirits. "For unclean spirits, crying with loud voice, came out of many that were possessed with them" (Acts 8:7). Paul expelled a demon from a girl in Acts 16. And in Acts 19, people would take handkerchiefs or aprons which had touched his body and were healed and set free from demons.

HEALING OF THE SICK

A woman who had been bleeding for twelve years touched Jesus' garment and "straightway the fountain of her blood was dried up; and she felt in her body that she was healed of that plague. And Jesus, immediately knowing in himself that *virtue had gone out of him*, turned him about in the press, and said, Who touched my clothes?" (Mark 5:29-30; emphasis added). Luke 6:19 also says, "And the whole multitude sought to touch him [Jesus]: *for there went virtue out of him*, and healed them all" (emphasis added).

The Greek word written for "virtue" is *dynamis*, which means miraculous power. Miraculous power left the body of Jesus and healed the sick woman and the whole multitude! In Acts 1:8, Jesus said that we would receive that same miraculous power when the Holy Spirit came upon us. One way we can be witnesses to Him after we receive the baptism is praying for the sick. What was it that healed the multitude and the woman? The power of God.

Post-Pentecost, Peter looked to a crippled man and said, "Silver and gold have I none; but such as I have give I thee: In the name of Jesus Christ of Nazareth rise up and walk" (Acts 3:6). Through Peter, Jesus healed a 40-year-old man paralyzed since birth and gave Peter the opportunity to preach the gospel. As a result, five thousand people got saved! God used this healing to bless this man and bring the gospel to many.

Philip prayed for the sick in Samaria, Ananias prayed for Paul to see, and Peter prayed for Aeneas who was paralyzed and bedridden for eight years, and Jesus healed them all. Peter prayed for a dead Tabitha to be raised up, and the Lord resurrected her. If you read the book of Acts, there are many more records of healing and miracles through the body of Christ on Earth. God used many of these healings and miracles to bring multitudes to salvation.

Just as there were sick people back then, there are sick people today. And just as there were people oppressed by demons back then, there are people oppressed by demons today. The casting out of demons did not disappear when the last apostle died, for even God didn't limit this to only the apostles. Philip wasn't an apostle but a deacon and God used him to cast out demons. More importantly, Jesus said in Mark 16 that one of the signs of those who would believe in Him *as a result* of the disciples preaching the gospel is the casting out of demons.

Jesus came to give us life, and life abundantly! We are His body on Earth and He cannot act without us. He is the head, and we are His hands and feet to the lost and those oppressed by the devil. We cannot do it without the power of the Holy Spirit and the name of Jesus Christ.

There may even come times when you will have to pray over yourself, spouse, children, or friends to be free from demonic oppression. I write this because I've seen it with my own eyes, and I've had to pray over myself to be set free through the name of Jesus. All glory to Him.

THE ONE WHO CONVICTS

In John 16:8-11, Jesus said, "And when he [the Holy Spirit] is come, he will reprove the world of sin, and of righteousness, and of judgment: Of sin, because they believe not on me; Of righteousness, because I go to my Father, and ye see me no more; Of judgment, because the prince of this world is judged."

Jesus declared that when the Holy Spirit comes, the Holy Spirit will convict the world of the three things: sin, righteousness, and judgment. He will convict the world of sin because they do not believe in Jesus. We see this come to fruition for the first time immediately after the outpouring of the Holy Spirit on the day of Pentecost.

Through Peter preaching the gospel, the Holy Spirit convicted 3,000 people of sin because they didn't believe in Jesus. We do not see this happen before Jesus poured out the Holy Spirit. There is no record of the disciples preaching the gospel after Jesus ascended and before the Holy Spirit came over them in Jerusalem.

The Holy Spirit will convict the world of righteousness,

because Jesus will go to the Father and the disciples would not see him until He came back. They would go on to preach about the righteousness of God without the physical Jesus anymore.

The Holy Spirit would come to convict the world of the righteousness of God and that Jesus is the Son of God even though He left Earth and returned to Heaven. "Blessed are they that have not seen, and yet have believed," said Jesus in John 20:29. Although many of us have never seen Him, we confess that Jesus is Lord by the Holy Spirit.

GOD'S PLAN FOR ALL BELIEVERS

Throughout history, many men and women lived for God without the baptism with the Holy Spirit. When they died, they went to be with the Lord, yet they missed out on their Father's wonderful gift to them. They missed out on a Helper, Comforter, and Teacher and God's complete plan for their lives. Perhaps in their ignorance or unbelief, they disobeyed Jesus' commandment to receive His baptism. However, for those who are still on this Earth, one is never too old to receive their Father's promise.

We live in the post-Pentecost era, where the gift of the Holy Spirit is available to all sons and daughters of

God. If the disciples who walked with the Son of God for three years were commanded to receive Him, how much more do we need Him?

7

EXTINGUISHING THE SPIRIT

"In all their affliction he was afflicted,
and the angel of his presence saved them:
in his love and in his pity he redeemed them;
and he bare them, and carried them
all the days of old. But they rebelled,
and vexed his holy Spirit: therefore
he was turned to be their enemy,
and he fought against them."

— ISAIAH 63:9-10

SOME PEOPLE MAY BELIEVE THAT WHEN A PERSON RE-
ceives the baptism with the Holy Spirit, they will
have free access to everything from Him any time
they desire. On the contrary, the Bible reveals that it is
possible for us to quench and grieve the Spirit of God,
and thus, dull His work in our lives. We cannot expect

the Spirit of God to move as He desires if we consistently partake in sin.

All sin and evil quenches the Spirit. The more we allow God to purify and prune us, the more room we give the Spirit of God to work through us. We must hold fast to what is good so that sin no longer muddies His voice and manifestation through us.

Paul wrote these instructions to the church: "Quench not the Spirit. Despise not prophesyings. Prove all things; hold fast that which is good" (1 Thess. 5:19-21). As we read in Joel and Acts, prophecy comes from the outpouring of the Holy Spirit. Sometimes we may encounter false prophets or people who believe they are prophesying but in reality, they are speaking empty words that will never come to fruition. In turn, we may turn away from the whole of prophecy. However if we reject the whole thing, we are rejecting the Holy Spirit's work on Earth.

A true prophet of God will not miss a word of God. If someone mistakes their thoughts and feelings for prophecy, it is their responsibility to know the difference. If they step out unsure, they should step back and know God's voice intimately as a sheep knows the voice of their shepherd.

The Bible declares that without love, prophecy is

nothing (1 Cor. 13:2). So, we must remember to keep things in the right priority. Paul wrote, "Follow after charity, and desire spiritual gifts, but rather that ye may prophesy" (1 Cor. 14:1). Instead of rejecting prophecies altogether, we must test all things and believe only the prophecies that come from the Spirit.

GRIEVING THE SPIRIT

"And grieve not the holy Spirit of God, whereby ye are sealed unto the day of redemption. Let all bitterness, and wrath, and anger, and clamour, and evil speaking, be put away from you, with all malice" (Eph. 4:30-31).

The first sin Paul lists as an offense to the Spirit of God is bitterness. Even if it sprouted ten years ago or yesterday, bitterness and unforgiveness hinders and grieves Him. In a parable, Jesus revealed the dreadful consequences of unforgiveness. "And his lord was wroth, and *delivered him to the tormentors*, till he should pay all that was due unto him. So *likewise shall my heavenly Father do also unto you*, if ye from your hearts forgive not every one his brother their trespasses" (Matt. 18:34-35). If we do not forgive from our hearts, our Father will deliver us into the tormentors. This can manifest in our lives in different ways such as physical illness or mental torment.

If you speak wrong and evil things, harbor bitterness, anger, complaints, and malice, go to the Lord and correct your ways. Be assured that the Holy Spirit will help you as you become more like Jesus for the glory of God. Make no mistake, these sins will hinder the work of the Spirit in your life.

You can still receive the baptism with the Spirit and speak in new tongues, but you will grieve Him and stop a lot He yearns to do in your life afterwards. Disobedience to God will stagnate you emotionally and spiritually for the rest of your life.

These actions oppose the fruits God desires us to bear. These fruits are "love, joy, peace, longsuffering, gentleness, goodness, faith, meekness, temperance" (Gal. 5:22-23). Love is supreme. God commands us to love one another; by loving one another, we will be known as Jesus' disciples. If we bear evil fruit, we grieve God's Spirit. How do we bear good fruit? We do it by obeying God's will.

Jesus said, "Ye shall know them by their fruits. Do men gather grapes of thorns, or figs of thistles? Every tree that bringeth not forth good fruit is hewn down, and *cast into the fire*. Not every one that saith unto me, Lord,

Lord, shall enter into the kingdom of heaven; *but he that doeth the will of my Father which is in heaven*. Many will say to me in that day, Lord, Lord, have we not prophesied in thy name? and in thy name have cast out devils? and in thy name done many wonderful works? And then will I profess unto them, I never knew you: depart from me, *ye that work iniquity*" (Matt. 7:16,19,21-23; emphasis added).

We will also be judged if we obey Him here on Earth. If we pray for others to be set free or prophesy, but we disobey Him by harboring bitterness and unforgiveness, we work iniquity. God is not impressed by our ministerial actions; He is pleased by our daily obedience to Him which few will see.

Let's read the next few verses in Ephesians 4 and 5. "And be ye kind one to another, tenderhearted, forgiving one another, even as God for Christ's sake hath forgiven you. Be ye therefore followers of God, as dear children; And walk in love, as Christ also hath loved us" (Eph. 4:32, 5:1-2). Walk in love and you will please the Spirit. We can forgive and love freely because God has forgiven us of our mountain of sins and loved us before we even knew Him and fought against Him.

If you are being convicted of your sins, it's a sign the

Holy Spirit is already working in your life. He needs to deal with these areas before He can use you to the full extent that He desires.

In the next few verses, Paul goes into more specifics, addressing fornication, uncleanness, covetousness, filthiness, foolish talking, and coarse jesting. The Bible says that no fornicator, unclean, or covetous person has any inheritance in God's kingdom. Ephesians 1 reveals that the promised Holy Spirit is the *guarantee* of our inheritance. Sin stops us from accessing our inheritance.

Galatians 5:16 says, "Walk in the Spirit, and ye shall not fulfil the lust of the flesh." When we partake in these aforementioned sins, the Holy Spirit cannot work freely or manifest His gifts purely in our lives. Like a clogged faucet with dirt and mire, little water will drip. But when we clean the faucet and filter, a rush of water will flow. The Holy Spirit is God—we should always look to please Him.

LYING TO THE SPIRIT

Acts 5 speaks of a man and his wife, Ananias and Sapphira, who sold a possession. Ananias kept some of the profit to himself, and brought another part to the apostles. When he lied to the apostles that he had given all of the profit to them, Peter told him that he hadn't lied to men, but to God.

When Ananias heard this, he immediately fell and died. When he lied to the church, he had lied to the Spirit of truth. His oblivious wife came hours later and like her husband before her, she lied. Then Peter questioned her. "How is it that ye have agreed together to *tempt the Spirit of the Lord?*" (Acts 5:9; emphasis added).

Sapphira fell dead immediately as well. Because they lied to the Spirit, they faced a fateful punishment. Notice how this did not happen under the old covenant, but under the new covenant of Jesus Christ's blood. When we lie to the Spirit of truth, we may face serious consequences.

INSULTING THE SPIRIT OF GRACE

The writer of Hebrew reveals that sinning willfully after you know the truth you insult the Spirit of grace (Heb. 10:26-31). We must *refuse* to count the blood of Jesus by which we are sanctified a common thing. If you know you've done this in the past (I know I have), confess and ask the Lord for forgiveness for He is faithful to forgive you.

Romans 6:1-2 says, "What shall we say then? Shall we continue in sin, that grace may abound? God forbid. How shall we, that are dead to sin, live any longer therein?"

When we abuse the grace God has so freely given to us, we insult the Spirit of grace. Be wise and do not do it.

The Lord gives grace to the humble. You will not be turned away if you admit your sins and turn away from them. Ask the Holy Spirit to help you in your weakness and He will. When we recognize areas of our lives that we must submit to God, we must not delay and do it immediately. If we don't, we will quiet the Spirit of God in our lives. The Lord must increase and we must decrease! The more we obey Him because we love Him, the more space we give the Spirit of God to work in us and through us for the glory of Jesus.

8

THE SEAL

"In whom ye also trusted,
after that ye heard the word of truth,
the gospel of your salvation:
in whom also after that ye believed,
ye were sealed with that holy Spirit of
promise,
Which is the earnest of our inheritance
until the redemption of the purchased
possession, unto the praise of his glory."

— Ephesians 1:13-14

THE WAY PAUL WORDED THE VERSE FEATURED ABOVE gives us a clue to a profound meaning behind the Father's promise. Note the specific words, "After that ye believed, ye were sealed with that holy Spirit of promise." It connects with Paul's question to the twelve disciples in Acts 19:2 which was, "Have ye received the

Holy Ghost since ye believed?"

Through Paul's question, the Bible shows that there is a separation between being saved and baptized with the Holy Spirit. For if a person received the baptism at the exact moment they believed in Christ, then Paul would have never asked them that question. He knew that there's an additional step after a person's salvation to step into everything God has for them.

Notice the word he used to describe the Holy Spirit in Ephesians. He called Him, "the holy Spirit of promise." That sounds quite familiar, doesn't it? As we've read earlier, the books of John, Luke, and Acts describe Jesus' baptism with the Holy Spirit as the Father's promise, the promised Holy Spirit, and as the word itself, "promise." The outpouring of the promised Holy Spirit brings forth two evidential signs: speaking in tongues and magnifying God.

So when a believer receives Jesus' baptism with the Holy Spirit, *then* they are sealed with the promised Holy Spirit. Being sealed is a separate event from salvation or in other words, God's ownership of you. For example, when a king seals his letter, it is already his letter in the first place. Nothing can ever change that. When he places his seal on his letter, he is only emphasizing and declaring that therein lies his great authority behind his words.

The seal adds power behind the letter and emphasizes and promotes his authority. So, when Jesus instructed the believers to wait in Jerusalem to receive power and thus, be sealed according to Ephesians 1, we must ask *why* He commanded them to receive it.

Great Power of God

After Jesus's body was placed in a tomb, the Pharisees and chief priests were afraid Jesus' disciples would come and steal it. So, they sought the Roman governor to ensure nothing of that sort would happen. With the governor's approval, the Jews sealed the tomb and placed guards. Behind the seal on Jesus' tomb stood the great power of Rome. It told anyone who set their eyes upon it that if they should dare break it, they would face Rome's cruel punishment.

In Luke 24 and Acts 1, Jesus declared that when believers received the baptism with the Holy Spirit, they would receive power. In a similar way, standing behind the seal of the Holy Spirit is the incomparable power of God. It is the same power that resurrected Jesus and set the church in heavenly places far above every name. And according to Jesus' words, when we receive the power of God, we can properly be witnesses to Him.

Paul, who had received the baptism with the Holy Spirit, wrote the following to the Thessalonians. "For our gospel came not unto you in word only, *but also in power, and in the Holy Ghost*, and in much assurance" (1 Thess. 1:5; emphasis added). Here Paul lists four non negotiable tools to preach the gospel: words, power, being in the Holy Spirit, and deep conviction. If Paul hadn't been baptized with the Spirit after he believed in the gospel, he would've not been able to preach the gospel in power.

Paul also wrote, "And my speech and my preaching was not with enticing words of man's wisdom, *but in demonstration of the Spirit and of power:* That your faith should not stand in the wisdom of men, *but in the power of God"* (1 Cor. 2:4-5; emphasis added). To preach the gospel or share the Word of God with someone, we must refuse to solely depend on compelling words. We need God's power, so that whoever may listen may not place their faith on our intelligence or eloquent skills.

His power manifests miracles and healings, but also as His invisible presence as we speak. Before Peter preached on that day of Pentecost, the unbelievers heard the believers speaking in their own languages and their curiosity opened the door to the gospel. Peter preached the gospel by simply sharing the Scriptures. The only different thing about Peter was that he had just received the baptism with the Holy Spirit. Only *after* he received it that he witnessed to thousands, for Jesus had promised him that once he was clothed with miraculous power that he would be His witness.

Just because we are saved doesn't mean that we carry *all* the necessary power of God to walk in what He has for us. The disciples and the other 100 believers (including Jesus' mother Mary and siblings) didn't possess all the power of God when they became saved. In fact, they lacked a vital amount of it before they received the baptism with the Holy Spirit. If that wasn't the case and we all receive the fullness of God when we are saved, then Jesus would have not commanded His believers to wait in Jerusalem to receive His power after He left.

When we are sealed by the promised Holy Spirit, the great power of God stands behind us. The invisible principalities and powers witness it and we can walk with more confidence on Earth.

Down Payment

Jesus said, "And, behold, I send the promise of my Father upon you: but tarry ye in the city of Jerusalem, until ye be *endued* with power from on high" (Luke 24:49; emphasis added). Endue is a transitive verb for endow. Webster's 1828 Dictionary defines endowed as, "Furnished with a portion of estate; supplied with a permanent fund."

Keeping that in mind, let's read where Paul described what happens when we receive Jesus' baptism. "Now he which stablisheth us with you in Christ, and hath anointed us, is God; Who hath *also sealed us*, and *given the earnest of the Spirit* in our hearts" (2 Cor. 1:21-22; emphasis added). Other translations call earnest a guarantee, down payment, or a pledge.

The blood of Christ has bought our redemption. We are saved, and a wonderful future lies beyond this world for us. The outpouring of the Holy Spirit is the guarantee of what He has for us. Many Christians have lived and died without this guarantee and are in Heaven with the Lord today. That's because our salvation doesn't rest on a sign or physical evidence, but on God's Word which speaks of Jesus' death and resurrection.

When we receive the baptism with the Holy Spirit, we are endowed with a portion of God's estate, which is His miraculous power. His promised Holy Spirit seals us, and we receive that power to be witnesses for the Lord. If fearful powers which stood behind a once famous kingdom such as Rome, how awe-striking is the power that stands behind a Spirit-filled believer.

9

OPEN THE GIFT

"Repent, and be baptized every one of you in the name of Jesus Christ for the remission of sins, and ye shall receive the gift of the Holy Ghost."

— ACTS 2:38

TO HAVE FAITH IS TO BELIEVE THE WORD OF GOD no matter the circumstances or symptoms around us. Without faith, it is impossible to please God. When we refuse to believe what God says in His Word, we dishonor Him.

One chief way to honor God is to believe His Word and act upon it. His Word is the foundation for our lives on Earth and beyond. God's promises—*when believed and acted upon*—are the pillars which hold the roof over our heads.

When Paul reprimanded the Christians in the province

of Galatia for falling back into works to be saved, he asked them if they received the Holy Spirit by works or by hearing of faith.

"Received ye the Spirit by the works of the law, or *by the hearing of faith?* . . . He [God] therefore that *ministereth* to you the Spirit, and *worketh miracles among you*, doeth he it by the works of the law, or *by the hearing of faith?*" (Gal. 3:2,5; emphasis added). According to Strong's Concordance, the Greek word for "minister" is *epichorégeó* which means to fully supply. Our Lord earnestly desires to *fully* supply us with His power, and we must obtain it by hearing of faith.

To receive the Spirit and see His miracles in our lives, we *must* possess faith. How does a person obtain faith? Romans 10:17 gives us the answer. "So then faith cometh by hearing, and hearing by the word of God."

The believers in Jerusalem received the Spirit by believing and obeying Jesus' commandment. Cornelius and his guests received Him by listening to God's Word preached through Peter. When we hear *and* believe the Word of God, it generates faith in our hearts. "For we walk by faith, not by sight" (2 Cor. 5:7). We believe what we *hear* from the Bible, not what we *see* around us.

Remember what the Word of God says of the baptism

with the Holy Spirit. In the same way you received your free gift of salvation, you can receive the Helper whom the Father promised to give you. When you heard the gospel preached concerning Jesus' death on the cross and resurrection, you believed even though you've never seen any of it. As eternal life is a gift you can only receive by faith, so is the Holy Spirit. You cannot struggle, strive, or beg to receive Him.

DEAD FAITH

James wrote, "What does it profit, my brethren, if some- one says he has faith but does not have works? Can faith save him? . . . Thou believest that there is one God; thou doest well: the devils also believe, and tremble. But wilt thou know, O vain man, *that faith without works is dead?* Was not Abraham our father justified by works, when he had offered Isaac his son upon the altar? Seest thou how faith wrought with his works, *and by works was faith made perfect?*" (James 2:14,19-23; emphasis added).

If you simply believe Jesus' baptism with the Holy Spirit is for you, believing is not enough. It's an internal and external matter. With your heart you believed God raised Jesus from the dead, and with your mouth, you confessed Jesus is Lord. *Then* you were saved! You acted upon the faith generated in your heart from hearing God's word about His salvation for you. You worked out your faith by speaking it out, bursting life into your dead faith, and therefore received eternal life.

What do you do in the matter of the baptism with the Holy Spirit? Confess with your mouth that you believe in the Father's promise. Tell Him that you believe that the outpouring of the Spirit is for you as well.

DIFFERENT WAYS HE COMES

As we read in the records of Acts, there are different ways a believer can receive the baptism. In the case of the Christians in Samaria, John the Baptist's twelve disciples, and even Paul himself, they had to have been prayed over to receive it. However, for the over 100 believers, the Eleven, and Cornelius and his guests, the Holy Spirit fell upon them when they believed God's Word. God doesn't limit Himself to one way.

In my testimony, I asked my father, who had received the baptism years earlier, to pray for me. I was sixteen and didn't fully understand what I was asking for, but God saw my heart and desire for Him. God didn't wait for perfection of knowledge. I believed that the Father's promise was for me and took a step of action by asking my father to pray for me.

Know that when we receive the outpouring of the Holy Spirit, it doesn't transform us into mature or perfect Christians. In fact, as we read in the Bible, most of the people who had received the gift of the Holy Spirit were freshly-born again Christians. The baptism is what we should receive at the *beginning* of our relationship with the Lord, but it does not make us automatically mature. In fact, as we read in Galatians, Paul had reprimanded the already Spirit-filled believers for slipping back into the laws of the old covenant.

The Father's promise is an amazing, necessary gift for us to grow in Him and bless others. We cannot reach our fullest spiritual potential without the Holy Spirit's help. We need Him to mature, but the matter is also conditional and dependent on us. We need to submit ourselves to Him and obey.

ASK HIM

When we read the beginning of Luke 11, we will see that when our Lord Jesus told His disciples to ask, knock, and seek, He was speaking of asking, knocking, and seeking for the Holy Spirit. In the beginning of the chapter, it starts off with the disciples asking to learn how to pray and Jesus giving them the Lord's Prayer. He explained the persistence of a friend asking for bread in the middle of the night and used it as an analogy for the disciples to ask, knock, and seek for the Holy Spirit.

Jesus finished His message by revealing the Father's desire for His children. "If ye then, being evil, know how to give good gifts unto your children: how much more shall your heavenly Father give the Holy Spirit *to them that ask him*?" (Luke 11:13; emphasis added).

Ask your Father in Heaven for the baptism with the Holy Spirit. He will pour Him upon you or will guide you to the right person to pray for you and pour Him upon you. The Holy Spirit will come and fill you, and you will begin to speak in a new language. The Bible doesn't say the believers on the day of Pentecost shouted in new languages, but rather that they *spoke* it. You will be in complete control for the Spirit of God is the Spirit of peace and order.

COME AND DRINK

As we've read earlier, Jesus promised us the following when speaking of the coming Holy Spirit. "If any man *thirst*, let him come unto me, *and drink*. He that believeth on me, as the scripture hath said, *out of his belly* shall flow rivers of *living water*. (But *this spake he of the Spirit* which they that believe on him should receive: for the Holy Ghost was not yet given; because that Jesus was not yet glorified.)" (John 7:37-39; emphasis added).

Jesus also likened the outpouring of the Spirit to living water when He told the Samaritan woman at the well, "If thou knewest the gift of God, and who it is that saith to thee, Give me to drink; thou woudest have asked of him, and he would have given thee *living water.* . . . Whosoever drinketh of this water shall thirst again: But whosoever drinketh of the water that *I shall give him* shall never thirst; but the water that *I shall give him* shall be *in* him a *well of water springing up into everlasting life*" (John 4:10,13-14; emphasis added). Jesus is the one who gives the Holy Spirit, because the Father gave the Holy Spirit to Him to pour out upon us.

"Therefore with joy shall ye draw water out of the

wells of salvation" (Isaiah 12:3). Our salvation through Christ gives us access to the living water God yearns to give us. Before Jesus walked on Earth, the Holy Spirit spoke through the mouth of Isaiah. "For *I will pour water* upon him that is *thirsty*, and floods upon the dry ground: *I will pour my spirit* upon thy seed, and my blessing upon thine offspring: And *they shall spring up as among the grass, as willows by the water courses*" (Isaiah 44:3-4; emphasis added). Life shall burst quickly and wonderfully when God's Spirit is poured out. Many will be brought to salvation, for a believer cannot witness properly without Jesus' baptism.

Paul wrote, "For by one Spirit are we *all baptized* into one body, whether we be Jews or Gentiles, whether we be bond or free; and have been all made to *drink into one Spirit*" (1 Cor. 12:13; emphasis added). God calls all believers to drink into one Holy Spirit through the Father's promise.

RECEIVE THE GIFT

When someone lays out a gift for you and tells you it's yours to take, do you look at them and beg for the gift? No, it would be a bizarre action and worse, it is the opposite of faith. Faith doesn't beg; it takes it now! You didn't beg to be saved, and you don't need to beg to be baptized. God's promised gift, the Holy Spirit, is resting on the table to be opened by you. If you believe, work out your faith by confessing it with your mouth.

Receive the Holy Spirit! Jesus is waiting. Go to Him, welcome Him to pour the Holy Spirit on you, and drink.

A PRAYER

Thank you Father for the great promise You gave us in the book of Joel, where You promised to pour out Your Spirit on all flesh. Your son Jesus Christ promised that after He returned to You that He would send the Holy Spirit upon us to be our Helper. I believe this promise is for me because I believe Jesus rose from the dead and I obey Him because He is my Lord and Savior.

Father, based on Your Word, I receive the infilling of Your Holy Spirit, which is the baptism You promised to me. I thank you that I will receive power when the Holy Spirit comes upon me so that I will be a witness to Jesus. Thank you for giving me a Helper and Guide here on Earth. May Jesus Christ receive all the glory through my life. In Jesus' name, amen.